PAULIST BIBLE STUDY PROGRAM

Paul, Missionary to the Gentiles

WORKBOOK

Workbook by	Mary Ann Getty
Video Scripts by	Anthony Tambasco
Prayers by	Maureen Crossen, R.S.M.

PAULIST PRESS

New York/Mahwah

Acknowledgements

Faith Sharing Principles are reprinted from RENEW, copyright © 1987 by the Roman Catholic Archdiocese of Newark, New Jersey. Used by permission.

Photographs courtesy of Lawrence Boadt, C.S.P.

Published by Paulist Press
997 Macarthur Blvd.
Mahwah, NJ 07430

Printed and bound in the United States of America.

Dear Friends,

It is a pleasure to present our new Paulist Bible Study Program. The Paulist Bible Study Program is designed to help adults understand the Bible in the light of contemporary biblical scholarship and to use the Bible as a source of prayer, reflection and action. It relates the study of the Bible to the liturgy, to the church, and to our daily lives. Those who long to know more about the Bible, based on the authentic Catholic tradition and the most responsible and best biblical scholarship, have a rich experience awaiting them.

Kevin A. Lynch, C.S.P.
Publisher

INTRODUCTION

Welcome to the Paulist Bible Study Program and to this second unit on the New Testament.

In this unit you will be introduced to the life and work of the apostle Paul, to his letters, and to those first communities of Christians which he addressed. This Workbook will serve as a reading guide to the Bible and to your companion text *Reading the New Testament* by Pheme Perkins. Each week it will point out what passages of the Bible you should read and what parts of the companion text are focused on these passages.

The Bible in the Life of the Church

The emergence of popular interest in the Bible among Catholics stems from the Second Vatican Council. Along with the new emphasis on the Scriptures during the Eucharist and other sacramental celebrations, the Council called upon all members of the church to grow in their knowledge and love of the Bible:

> Just as the life of the church grows through persistent participation in the eucharistic mystery, so we may hope for a new surge of spiritual vitality from intensified veneration for God's word (*Decree on Revelation*, 26).

The vision of the central place of the Scriptures which the Council set forth is becoming more and more a reality.

The church has always venerated the divine Scriptures just as she venerates the body of the Lord, since from the table of both the word of God and of the body of Christ she unceasingly receives and offers to the faithful the bread of life, especially in the sacred liturgy. She has always regarded the Scriptures together with sacred tradition as the supreme rule of faith, and will ever do so. (*Decree on Revelation,* 21).

Our hope is that this program will be yet another resource which will take the process of integrating Scripture into the life of the Church one step further.

Jesus' Own Bible Study Model

In 1986, Archbishop Roger Mahoney of Los Angeles issued a pastoral letter entitled "The Bible in the Life of the Church." One part of the letter reflects on Jesus' own approach to teaching the Scriptures to his disciples as he walked with two of them on the road to Emmaus (Luke 24:13-35). Archbishop Mahoney's reflections on this passage are a fitting introduction to our study of the Bible.

The two disciples are on their way from Jerusalem to Emmaus when Jesus—his appearance hidden—joins them. He responds to their bewilderment by "interpreting for them every passage of Scripture which referred to him." This was the most clear example of Jesus sharing the Scriptures that we find in the gospels. For our own Bible study to be beneficial, then, we too must open our hearts and lives to allow Jesus to unlock the meaning of his message for us.

But two additional elements in the Emmaus journey are also required to validate our own experience of the Scriptures. First, our Scripture study must lead towards, center around, and flow from the Eucharist—the Mass. It was only in "the breaking of the bread" that the full meaning of Jesus' explanations became clear to the two men journeying to Emmaus. As Catholics, we too must always focus our Bible studies in and through the Eucharist. And secondly, we must be guided in our Scripture studies through "Simon Peter—the church." Recall that the two men returned in haste to Jerusalem where they were greeted with: "The Lord has been raised! It is true! He has appeared to Simon." This validation by Peter—by the church—is essential to our authentic understanding of the word of God.

The Importance of Commitment

What are your goals for your participation in this program? As you begin, take a few moments to reflect upon your goals and jot them down. These may involve gaining some knowledge, but don't omit other possible gains such as growing in your spirituality or prayer life, building community within your parish. Any goal worth achieving requires commitment. During this program you are invited to make a commitment to grow in your understanding and appreciation of the Bible.

All commitments require time. In this case, you are committing yourself to be present at the eight sessions and to participate in the learning process. This will require the most precious of commodities: time.

What follows is a description of the various steps you should take to prepare for and to follow-up on a meeting. Only you can determine how much time you have to spend on these steps. Not everything needs to be done now. Hopefully, the Paulist Bible Study Program will provide you with the resources to continue your own study well after a particular unit ends.

In addition to a time commitment, you are making a commitment to the other participants in your group. You bring unique gifts and experience to this study of the Bible that will enrich your co-learners. The steps below offer some tips on how you can both share your own insights and enable others to share theirs.

Preparing for the Meeting

Each week you will be meeting with others to reflect on the Scriptures and the parts of the companion text. Before you engage in the exercises in this book, follow the steps outlined for each session in the section called Preparation.

1. Prayerfully read the appointed Bible passages. Here is a simple way to do that:

2. Read the assigned portion of the companion text. You may want to read a little bit each day to coordinate with your prayerful reading of the Bible. Many find it helpful to mark the text for key parts or to jot down questions that may arise during a reading.

3. Read the Focus and Review of Contents before the meeting. If you have time, try to work on responses to the review questions. Your companion text also has review questions after each chapter which will be helpful.

During the Meeting

Each session is designed to last two hours. Here are the steps for each session and some suggestions on how to make use of them.

Opening Prayer (5 minutes)
Place yourself and your group in God's presence, asking for the guidance of the Holy Spirit during the upcoming session.

Review of Contents (25 minutes)
This section gives you the opportunity to express what you have learned and to learn from the insights of others. If you have questions other than those raised in the review, bring them up at this time. While your Program Leader cannot be ex-

pected to have all the answers, he or she may be able to help you find an answer to your question.

Video (20 minutes)

The video is designed to enrich your learning by providing the visual dimension of what you are studying. Before viewing the program, look at the highlight questions. Jot down the answers as you watch the program. Afterwards, there is a brief time for your to raise questions or make a comment.

Learning Activity (25 minutes)

During this segment, you will work with others in an exercise to further integrate the meaning of the Scripture you have read and to apply it to your life.

Faith Sharing (25 minutes)

The following suggestions, borrowed from RENEW, are helpful guidelines for faith sharing:

- The entire faith-sharing process is seen as prayer, i.e., listening to the word of God as broken by others' experience.
- Constant attention to respect, honesty and openness for each person will assist the group's growth.
- Each person shares on the level where he/she feels comfortable.
- Silence is a vital part of the total process of faith sharing. Participants are given time to reflect before any sharing begins, and a period of comfortable silence might occur between individual sharings.
- Persons are encouraged to wait to share a second time until others who wish to do so have contributed.
- The entire group is responsible for participating and faith sharing.
- Confidentiality is essential, allowing each person to share honestly.
- Reaching beyond the group in action and response is essential for the growth of individuals, the group and the church.

Closing Prayer (10 minutes)

Having shared our faith together, we conclude with prayer. Join in the spirit of the prayer service by singing, praying, and listening to the word of God.

After the Meeting

Journaling

For each session, one or more journal idea is suggested. You may wish to keep a journal either to do these exercises, or simply to write your own reflections.

Additional Resources

Each week a number of sources are referred to for further reading and study. Your parish may have purchased these books for a parish resource library or you may obtain them from Paulist Press. Your program leader has further information. You may wish to consult these sources for continued study after the unit ends.

1. An Introduction to Paul

FOCUS

Many of us know about Paul only from the readings we hear at the liturgy. These are short excerpts from his letters and are heard outside of the context of the particular letter as a whole. Because Paul's personality comes through so strongly in his letters, many of us also have some strong feelings about Paul, both positive and negative. This unit of the Paulist Bible Study Program will give us the opportunity to learn more about Paul and to test how true our initial impressions of him are.

In this session we will reflect on the knowledge and experience we bring to this study of Paul. In the video, we will get an overview of Paul's life and the sources available to us for knowing about it: the Acts of the Apostles and Paul's own letters. We will also learn about the nature, purpose and structure of Paul's letters. Finally, we will reflect together on Paul's experience of being called to be an apostle and share together how we experience God calling us.

OPENING PRAYER

Call to Prayer

Leader: (while lighting the candle)
We wish you the grace and peace of God our Father and
the Lord Jesus Christ, to whom be glory for ever and
ever. Amen.

Paul Speaks to Us

Let us pray:
(The hymn from Col 1:12-20 may be prayed in unison or
each participant may pray a verse in turn.)

Let us give thanks to God
for having made us worthy
to share the lot of the saints in light.

God rescued us
from the power of darkness
and brought us
into the kingdom of his beloved Son.
Through him we have redemption,
the forgiveness of our sins.

He is the image of the invisible God,
the first-born of all creatures.
In him everything in heaven and on earth was created,
things visible and invisible.

All were created through him;
all were created for him.
He is before all else that is.
In him everything continues in being.

It is he who is head of the body, the church!
He who is the beginning,
the first-born of the dead,
so that primacy may be his in everything.

It pleased God to make absolute fullness reside in him
and, by means of him, to reconcile everything in his
      person,
both on earth and in the heavens,
making peace through the blood of his cross.

Prayer

All:
God of life, we give you thanks for the wonders of your
works. Open our minds and hearts now to the revelation
of your presence through your teacher, Paul. We ask this
in the name of Jesus Christ our Risen Lord. Amen.

GETTING STARTED

1. Call to mind what you already know of Paul's life and
jot down some ideas. The following questions may be
helpful.

Who is Paul?

When did he become a follower of Christ?

What did he do?

How do we know about him?

Did he know Jesus during his earthly ministry?

Was he an apostle?

Why is he so important in Christian history?

Are there any passages from Paul's writings that stand out as you begin to think about him?

2. In your small group, share your responses to these questions:

What do you think about Paul?
Do you "like" him or not?
Why?

3. Spend a few moments writing your personal learning goals for this unit of the Paulist Bible Study Program. (You may wish to return to this and give it more thought after the conclusion of this session.)

My learning goals for this study of Paul are:

VIDEO

An Introduction to Paul

As you view this program, make note of the following:

1. What are the three sources for our information about Paul?

a) _____

b) _____

c) _____

2. Why must we use the Acts of the Apostles cautiously as a source for Paul's life?

_____

_____

3. Complete the sentences below:

Paul was born in _____, a prosperous and cultured Gentile city.

He was raised a _____ and was trained as a _____.

He was converted to Christianity near the city of _____ around the year _____.

According to Acts, Paul made _____ missionary journeys.

He died in _____ around the year _____.

BREAK
(10 minutes)

LEARNING ACTIVITY

1. The New Testament arranges Paul's letters according to length, from the longest to the shortest. Letters to communities are placed before letters to individuals. The thirteen letters ascribed to Paul are listed below in their order of appearance in the New Testament. However, biblical scholars today agree that probably only seven were actually written or dictated by Paul. Using the chronology of Paul's life found on page 139 of Perkins, check the seven authentic letters of Paul and record the approximate date for each.

Romans
1 Corinthians
2 Corinthians
Galatians
Ephesians
Philippians
Colossians
1 Thessalonians
2 Thessalonians
1 Timothy
2 Timothy
Titus
Philemon

2. Paul's letters follow the three-part structure of a Greek letter: introduction, body, and conclusion.

The introduction usually contains a greeting identifying the sender and the addressees, and a thanksgiving.

The body contains the doctrine or teaching and usually some exhortation or encouragement that Christians conduct themselves in a certain way. The Greek word used to describe such an exhortation is *paranesis*. This exhortation is based on the Christians' common acceptance of the doctrine.

The conclusion contains travel plans, personal greetings and oftentimes instructions that the letter be read to the whole local church.

Working with other members of your small group under the direction of your leader, identify the major parts of one or more of the following letters. Refer to the outlines of these letters in your companion text.

Philemon (page 148)
1 Thessalonians (page 152)
2 Thessalonians (page 152-3)
Philippians (page 157)
Galatians (page 165)
Romans (page 171)

Letter:

Introduction:

Body:

Conclusion:

3. Paul's letters provided guidance in situations where Paul himself could not be present. The letters were a kind of substitute for Paul's own presence. They were deli-

vered by a trusted messenger or companion of Paul and were read to the whole community.

Read one or two of the following passages and then answer the questions appropriate to the passages read:
a. 1 Cor 1:1-3; 16:1-4, 10-12, 19-24
b. Phil 1:1-2; 4:1-3, 21-23
c. Phlm 1-3, 23-25
d. 2 Cor 13:10-13

1) Is there any instruction in this passage? If so, what is it?

2) Is anyone mentioned as Paul's messenger? Does he name any co-authors? Who acts as Paul's representative in the church he addresses?

3) Is there any evidence in this passage that Paul's letter was intended not only for individuals but for the whole church?

FAITH SHARING

1. Like us, Paul did not know the earthly Jesus. It was his encounter and ongoing relationship with the risen Jesus which made his faith real, deep and contagious for others.

In your group, read aloud Gal 1:11-24 and 2:19-20—passages in which Paul expresses his faith experience. On the basis of this reading, reflect on and share with members of your group your responses to the following questions:

How does Paul describe his calling?

What does he understand as his mission?

What does it mean for him to be a Christian?

How were you called to be a believer?

What is your mission?

What does it mean for you to be a Christian?

CLOSING PRAYER

Hearing the Word

Leader:
Like Paul, we too are called to God through our personal experiences. Let us listen to God's word through Paul as we contemplate the gift God reveals through our lives.

Reading
1 Cor 12:12-21, 27

Sharing Our Light

Leader:
Let us give thanks to God for calling us to share our gifts like light to the world. I invite you to take a candle, light it from the candle by the Bible, and offer a prayer of thanksgiving to God for a gift you have received.

Leader:
Let us stand and raise our gifts before God.
(Participants stand and raise candles)
God, we give you thanks for the gifts you give freely. Help us to see these gifts as signs of your presence in the church. Bless these gifts in us that they may enlighten us to see the needs of others. We ask this in the name of Jesus, the fire of your love and light of the world.

All:
Amen.

Thessalonica was visited by Paul on his second missionary journey. This modern street was built over the Via Egnatia, *the Roman road on which Paul would have traveled. The arch of Galerius was erected in 297 A.D.*

FOLLOW-UP

A. Journaling

Read 1 Cor 9:16-27 and 2 Cor 4:1-2, 7-11, 16. Write a prayer or reflection in which you give thanks for your call and mission. Reflect upon your own experiences of mercy and healing. Are there areas in which you need to stress God's saving power more than your own unworthiness or worthiness?

B. Additional Resources

1. Read Gal 1:11-24 and 2 Cor 12:7-10 in which Paul describes his call. Then read Acts 9 where Luke describes Paul's conversion. What are some of the differences you see when you compare Paul and Luke?

2. Read Pheme Perkins, *Reading the New Testament*, Chapter 8, "The Life of Paul," pp. 135-147.

3. Read Joseph P. Fitzpatrick, S.J. *Paul, Saint of the Inner City*, pp. 1-20.

4. Read *The Catholic Study Bible*, "Paul and His Writings," RG 470-472.

5. a. Using the Hammond *Atlas of the Bible Lands*, examine the maps on pp. 32-33 which trace the missionary journeys of Paul. Compare the distance Jesus traveled (from Nazareth to Jerusalem) and Paul's travels. This comparison may help you to understand why Paul had such an impact on the early church.

b. Locate the cities which Paul addresses in his letters. What do they have in common? Where is Galatia and how is it different from the other destinations?

c. Locate Tarsus (Paul's birth city), Damascus (his destination when he first encountered Christ, according to Luke) and Jerusalem (where Paul hoped to bring believers in Christ to trial). What do you suppose is the significance of returning Christians to Jerusalem for trial?

2. Paul's World and the Letter to Philemon

Preparation

- Read the Letter to Philemon.
- Read Perkins, Chapter 7, "The World of Paul," pp. 114-134 and Chapter 8 on Philemon, pp. 147-150.
- Try to read as many of the references mentioned in the text as you have time for.
- For the mixed social status of the early Christians and Paul's language of community, topics which will be the focus of learning activities in this session, see the following:
  — rich and poor: 1 Cor 1:26-29
  — women and men, married and unmarried: Rom 16 and see notes in NAB; Phlm 1-3; 1 Cor 1:11; 7:1, 8, 12, 25-28
  — slaves and free: 1 Cor 7:21-22
  — Jews and Gentiles: Gal 3:28-29; Rom 1:16-17
  — artisans, merchants, craftsmen: 1 Thess 4:9-12; 2 Thess 3:8-11
  — the ecclesia, or church: 1 Cor 1:2; 2 Cor 1:1; Phil 1:1
  — examples of familial language used by Paul: Rom 9:1-5; 11:25; 1 Thess 2:7-11
- Reflect on the FOCUS statement and REVIEW OF CONTENTS questions.

FOCUS

If we reflect on our experience of belonging to a group, we will recognize that there are two dynamics present in all groups. People come together to achieve some goal, and they develop relationships among each other in the process. This dynamic is present in the church, both today and in the time of Paul.

That is why Paul always had at least two goals in mind while writing to the Christians at various locations. First, he tried to develop community life, to form a cohesive society among members of the community from different backgrounds. Second, he tried to give guidelines about how the particular church could fulfill its mission and survive in an alien world among competing religions and philosophies.

In this session we will consider the complex world in which the first churches developed. It was a world of Jews and Gentiles, rich and poor, slaves and free. Those who heard or read Paul's letters were people familiar with a variety of religions and religious symbols, who dabbled in philosophy and probably believed in the power of magic and such sciences as astrology. In the video we will learn more about these religions and philosophies.

We will also study how Paul sought to build up the unity of these churches. Paul wrote to churches in crisis situations. Behind each letter there was a "story." Understanding these stories is the key to understanding Paul. In this session we will learn the story behind Philemon. Finally, we will share our faith on how we, like the first Christians, are called to live our common baptism.

OPENING PRAYER

Call to Prayer

Leader:
I, _____, a witness for Christ Jesus, greet this church which gathers here (name parish or host). Grace to you and peace from God our Father and from the Lord Jesus Christ.

All:
And also to you.

Reading
Rom 6:3-6

Paul Speaks to Us

Leader:
God of Hope, through baptism you call us to rise to new ways of life. As your people gathered here, bless us as we continue our search for knowledge of you and give us the courage to be your body through our service. We ask this through the grace of our Lord Jesus Christ and the Holy Spirit,

All:
Amen.

"Greeks look for wisdom . . ." (1 Cor 1:22). This is the philosopher Chryssipus of the third century B.C.

REVIEW OF CONTENTS

1. For Paul, it was the common baptism which Christians share that changed the ways in which they were to relate to one another and to society. It was also the basis for resolving moral dilemmas in the church. The letter to Philemon is an example of how Paul's letters can serve as a model for understanding this aspect of Paul's theology of baptism.

a) Philemon is a fairly informal letter, yet the three divisions of a classic Greek letter can be distinguished here. Name them and identify the appropriate verses.

b) What are the ways in which Paul alludes to Christians' interdependence in this letter?

c) Reread Philemon and identify three ways in which Philemon is indebted or subject to Paul. Why does Paul insist on this?

d) What does Paul ask of Philemon? How clearly does he express this? What follow-up does Paul promise?

2. a) Is there any indication in Philemon that Paul wants to reform all of society and abolish slavery?

b) What is the basis in "doctrine" or "Christian teaching" that Paul suggests should affect Philemon's behavior toward Onesimus?

c) What indications are there in Philemon that Paul's letter had impressive authority within the community?

VIDEO

The World of Paul

As you view the video, please make note of the following:

1. Paul adapted Christianity from its _____ setting to an _____ culture.

2. What does the video present as the motto of each of these ancient philosophies?

a. Platonism

_____

b. Stoicism

_____

c. Epicureanism

_____

BREAK
(10 minutes)

LEARNING ACTIVITY

The letters of Paul tell us a great deal about the life of the early church: about its worship, its beliefs, its moral teaching, its daily life and its problems. They highlight the need for cohesiveness or community among Christians.

1. Read one of the following groups of passages aloud in your group (your leader may assign one to you). How is the life of Christians described as distinct from the life of people in ordinary society?

a. 1 Cor 1:4-17, 26—2:8; 3:18-23
b. Rom 12:1-4, 14-21; 14:1-3, 13-18
c. 1 Thess 1:2-10; 2:13-16; 3:9-13
d. Phil 1:27-2:11; 4:1-9

2. Relying on your reading and review of Perkins, the video presentation, the specific New Testament references you have just read, and your imagination, construct a profile of the New Testament community on which you focused in question 1 (i.e., Rome, Corinth, Thessalonica, or Philippi).

You might begin, "I am a single Gentile woman in the community at Corinth . . ." or "I am a Jewish Christian of a noted family living in Philippi . . ." and proceed to describe the life of that particular community. If you describe the community from the perspective of an individual person, you might include how baptism has changed his or her thinking, relationships, behavior, etc.

FAITH SHARING

1. As with the early Christians, our common baptism involves a responsibility: to live our beliefs, and to practice what we profess. For Paul, the experiences of his life were a source to strengthen and exhort others. For Philemon, leadership in the church included taking concrete risks in the way he conducted business, lived his family life, and exercised authority.

What does your baptism mean to you?

What kind of social responsibility do you think it requires?

Share one way you try to live this.

2. Which aspect of Paul's own example is most impressive or persuasive for you. Why?

CLOSING PRAYER

Baptismal Renewal

Reader:
Our common baptism challenges us to change our thinking and behavior by participating in God's transforming power which restores grace where sin had prevailed, and life where there was death.

Reader:
Paul assures us that our hope in God will not be disappointed, because the love of God has been poured out in our hearts through the Holy Spirit who has been given to us.

Invitation for Blessing

Leader:
As a reminder of our baptism, a sign of our mission, let us place a sign of the cross on each other's foreheads with this water. If you would like to offer a prayer for the person beside you in thanksgiving for his/her works of service or for encouragement to continue in faith, please feel free to do so.

Shared Prayer

Leader:
Let us offer our prayers for the local and universal church and its mission.

Let us conclude our prayers with the words Jesus gave us: Our Father . . . .

FOLLOW-UP

A. Journaling

Consider your baptism as a daily invitation to integrate more honestly your beliefs and your behavior. Write a short letter in the style of Philemon to yourself or to someone you know well in which you extend a challenge to such integrity of faith and morality. Include such motivations as your own experience of mercy and healing, the various ways in which you and your addressee are interdependent, some suggestions for changes that can be made.
OR
Write a prayer or meditation in which you acknowledge discrepancies between your faith and your daily behavior and the need for grace to eliminate these discrepancies.

B. Additional Resources

1. Read Philemon in *The Catholic Study Bible*, ''Philemon,'' RG 538-540.

2. Consult the maps in the Hammond *Atlas of the Bible Lands*, p. 33. Find Colossae where Philemon was a leader of a church community. Locate Thessalonica and Philippi, destinations of the letters we will study in the next session.

3. Thessalonians and Philippians

Preparation

- Read Perkins, Chapter 8, "Missionary to the Gentiles," pp. 150-159
- Read 1 Thessalonians and Philippians; also read 2 Thessalonians 2:1-12; Acts 16:11-40 and 17:1-9
- Try to read as many references mentioned in the text as you have time for. The following will be the focus of the learning activities this session:
  — Paul's gratitude for the faith and love of these communities: 1 Thess 1:2-3; 2:17—3:6; Phil 4:10-14
  — Encouragement in the midst of disillusionment: 1 Thess 4:13-18
  — Concern about the "Day of the Lord": 1 Thess 4:17; 5:1-11; 2 Thess 2:1-12; Phil 2:12-13; 3:18-21
  — Christians are to be a model for others to respect and imitate: 1 Thess 4:11-12; 2 Thess 3:6-13; Phil 1:27—2:4; 2:14-18
- Reflect on the FOCUS statement and REVIEW OF CONTENTS questions.

FOCUS

Probably all of us can identify certain persons—pastors, teachers, mentors—whose words and lives have been a source of inspiration to us. We have seen that Paul was a passionate and courageous leader. Few seemed able to remain indifferent to him. He had strong opponents and loyal friends. Paul was a dynamic and tireless missionary. His zeal to evangelize the Gentiles compelled him to keep moving further into Gentile territory. Yet his impact continued to be felt and he was eager to maintain contact with the churches he left behind.

The letters to the Thessalonians and Philippians reveal a remarkable affection between Paul and the Christians there. In 1 Thessalonians, the earliest letter we have from Paul, the apostle expresses gratitude for their faith and says it provides encouragement to other communities. Paul and the Thessalonians envision a short-term future which they believe will culminate soon in Christ's victorious return to judge the world. Paul admonishes them to remain steadfast in faith and to build up community.

Philippians (along with Philemon, Ephesians and Colossians) is one of four "captivity epistles," so-called because Paul writes them from prison. Written near the end of Paul's life, from either Ephesus or Rome, Philippians reveals a calmer Paul, an apostle who is beginning to understand that the end may not come for a while and that the church may endure for a long time. Even in the midst of continued, indeed heightened suffering, the terms occurring most frequently in Philippians are, paradoxically, "community" and "joy."

In this session we will see Paul the pastor in relationship to two of his most successful communities. Paul tries to encourage the Christians in Thessalonica and Philippi to resist discouragement and to become a model for others to follow as Paul himself is a model for them.

These remains of the Roman theatre at Philippi attest to the Roman character of the city.

OPENING PRAYER

Call to Prayer

Leader:
Grace and peace be yours from God the Father and the Lord Jesus Christ.

All:
And also with you.

Paul Speaks to Us

The hymn from Philippians 2:5-11 may be prayed together or each member of the group may pray one verse.

Have among yourselves the same attitude that is also
    yours in Christ Jesus,

Who, though he was in the form of God,
did not regard equality with God something to be
    grasped.

Rather, he emptied himself, taking the form of a slave,
    coming in human likeness; and found human in ap-
    pearance,
he humbled himself, becoming obedient to death,
even death on a cross.

Because of this God greatly exalted him
and bestowed on him the name that is above every name,
that at the name of Jesus, every knee should bend,
of those in heaven and on earth and under the earth,
and every tongue confess that Jesus Christ is Lord,
to the glory of God the Father.

Leader:
As we continue our study of Paul, may God continue to open our lives to this gospel of Jesus Christ, and strengthen us to carry out the good works that flow from us when our attitude is that of Jesus Christ.

All:
Amen.

REVIEW OF CONTENTS

1. Identify the following persons connected with the churches in Thessalonica and Philippi and share as much information as you can about these people. If you need further help, use the notes of the New American Bible (NAB).

Timothy: Acts 16:1-5; Phil 1:1; 2:19-24; Thess 1:1; 2 Thess 1:1; 1 Tim 1:1-2; 4:6-16

Jason: Acts 17:5-9

Silas (or Silvanus?): Acts 15:40-41; 17:4, 15

Lydia: Acts 16:11-15, 38-40

Euodia, Syntyche, Clement: Phil 4:2-4

Epaphroditus: Phil 2:25-30; 4:18

2. The return of Christ is designated by the Greek term, *parousia*, meaning "coming." The earliest image of Christ's return was that he would come victoriously, to judge the world.

a. In his letter to the Thessalonians, what does Paul say about the return of Christ?

b. Why are the Thessalonians so disturbed by the death of some of their members?

c. Why might death have been a different kind of a faith problem for the first Christians than it is for us today?

3. Why does charity play such a prominent role in Paul's letters to the Thessalonians and Philippians?

4. Suffering is an important theme of these epistles. In what contexts does Paul speak of suffering? To whose suffering does Paul allude?

5. Paul wrote Philemon and Philippians from prison.

a. What indications for this are there in these letters? How do you think this situation affected Paul's message?

b. Can you detect any evidence of development in Paul's thinking about suffering and about the *parousia* if you compare Thessalonians with Philippians?

6. In Philippians, Paul refers to Judaizers or those who are trying to impose restrictions of the Jewish law on the Gentiles who are converting to Christ. He says that they are concerned only with the "flesh" and not the spirit.

a. Read Phil 3:2-11, 19-21. Paul attributes certain practices to the "flesh." To which practices is he referring?

b. What distinctions of the "flesh" could Paul himself boast about?

VIDEO

The Churches of Thessalonica and Philippi

As you view the video, please make note of the following:

1. Who does Luke say is with Paul as he enters into Greece on his second missionary journey?

_____

_____

2. What does the video say about the social and religious background of Thessalonica?

_____

_____

3. What does the video say about the social and religious background of Philippi?

_____

_____

BREAK
(10 minutes)

LEARNING ACTIVITY

In small groups, reflect on one or more (as time allows) of the issues which confronted the churches of Thessalonica or Philippi. Answer the following questions for each issue:

How does Paul address the problem?
Do we experience problems of this sort today?
How does Paul's advice apply to us?

1 Thessalonians

a) The death of Christians and the delay of the *parousia* (4:13—5:11)

b) Persecution (2:14-16)

c) Church order (4:9-12; 5:12-22)

Philippians

a) Disunity in the community (2:1-4; 4:1-3)

b) The challenge of suffering, especially that due to persecution by others (1:27-30; 3:17-21)

c) Problems with Judaizers (3:2-4)

FAITH SHARING

1. Read the Christ-hymn of Phil 2:5-11. The first part of the hymn has to do with Christ's self-emptying (vv. 6-8) and the last with exaltation (vv. 9-11). With other members of your small group, share some ideas on the following:

a. What are ways Christ "emptied" himself?

b. What are some ways in which you as a Christian are called to "empty yourself" in today's world?

c. What are the ways in which God exalted Jesus?

d. In your efforts to imitate Jesus' self-emptying, do you experience anything that you would call God exalting you?

CLOSING PRAYER

Hearing the Word

Leader:
As Paul was called to address the crises and challenges of his time, let us bring to mind the crises and challenges in the church and in the world that demand our faith and response.

Silent Prayer

Reading
Phil 1:13-20

(Brief pause)

Leader:
Let us offer our needs and suffering to God. The response to our prayer is: "God of hope, hear us."

Shared Prayer

Leader:
God of Our Lord Jesus Christ, in baptism we were saved, through our gifts you shine in our world. May our baptism and our gifts be for us the courage and the power by which we confront the challenges and suffering in our church and world. Keep safe this day (night) all those whose lives are threatened because of their work for the gospel and for justice. We ask this in Jesus' name, and in the power of your Holy Spirit.

All:
Amen.

Blessing
(All stand and extend hands in sign of blessing.)

Leader:

May the God of peace make you perfect in holiness (1 Thess 5:23).

All:

Amen.

Leader:

May God preserve you whole and entire, spirit, soul and body, irreproachable at the coming of our Lord Jesus Christ (1 Thess 5:23).

All:

Amen.

Leader:

May you be found rich in the harvest of justice which Jesus Christ has ripened in you, to the glory and praise of God (Phil 1:11).

All:

Amen.

FOLLOW-UP

A. Journaling

Read 1 Thess 1:2-10. Consider the ways in which daily conversion to the Christian life means surrendering false idols and turning to worship the "living God." What are some of your "idols" and what does it mean to you to think of God as the "living God"? Name some idols in your own life that you have learned to relinquish in your pursuit of the living God. Are there others you can imagine will need to be surrendered? Write a prayer or reflection acknowledging your willingness to be more deeply converted. Are there also behaviors that you need to change?

B. Additional Resources

1. Joseph P. Fitzpatrick, S.J. *Paul: Saint of the Inner City*, Chapter 3, "Thessalonica," pp. 32-38.

2. Read *The Catholic Study Bible*, articles on 1 and 2 Thessalonians and on Philippians, RG 522-533 and RG 514-518. Also read the introductions to these books in this or another New American Bible.

3. Using the Hammond *Atlas of the Bible Lands*, pp. 32-33, locate Thessalonica and Philippi in the province of Macedonia. How far apart are they? How many times did Paul visit each? On which journeys? Find Corinth and picture Paul living and working there, writing 1 Thessalonians back to that community he had recently established. The Corinthian community will be the subject for our next two sessions.

4. 1 Corinthians

Preparation

- Read Perkins, Chapter 10, "Divisions in Corinth," pp. 175-186; study the outline on p. 185.
- Read Acts 18 and 1 Corinthians.
- Reflect on the FOCUS statement and REVIEW OF CONTENTS questions.

The remains of the Roman forum in Corinth, with Acro-Corinth in the background.

FOCUS

Paul's relationship with the Corinthians was complex. He had lived and worked among them longer than with any other community we know of, and yet the Corinthians were very critical of him. The urban society of Corinth provided a unique challenge to Paul's preaching. Corinthians were extremely competitive, even where spiritual gifts were concerned. Paul tried to reverse their priorities by preaching the "wisdom of the cross." Further, many conflicts existed within the Corinthian community, probably because of the diverse backgrounds of the Christians there. In the first letter to the Corinthians, Paul coins the phrase the "Body of Christ" which he uses in several different contexts to show that Christians must develop a new way of relating to one another.

In this session we will study 1 Corinthians to see how Paul struggles to help the Corinthians see themselves as a new creation, the body of Christ. The video will provide us with a look at the complexity of the community and Paul's relationship to them. We will also explore how Paul's advice to this church in resolving their problems can be helpful to us today.

OPENING PRAYER

Call to Prayer

Leader:
May the grace and peace of God our Father and the Lord Jesus Christ be with you.

All:
And also with you.

Paul Speaks to Us

Paul's words from 1 Cor 1:18-24 may be recited together or by alternate halves of the group.

For the word of the cross is folly to those who are perishing, but to us who are being saved it is the power of God.

For it is written, "I will destroy the wisdom of the wise, and the cleverness of the clever I will thwart."

Where is the wise one? Where is the scribe? Where is the debater of this age? Has not God made foolish the wisdom of the world?

For since, in the wisdom of God, the world did not know God through wisdom,

it pleased God through the folly of what we preach to save those who believe.

For Jews demand signs and Greeks seek wisdom, but we preach Christ crucified, a stumbling block to Jews and folly to Gentiles.

But to those who are called, both Jews and Greeks, Christ the power of God and the wisdom of God.

Leader:
Let us pray. (Pause.) God, whose weakness is stronger than human strength, help us to see our weakness as openness to you. Draw us through our weakness to humbly serve you in the poor, in the sick and in the unwanted. We ask this in the name of our crucified and risen savior, Jesus Christ.

All:
Amen.

REVIEW OF CONTENTS

1. In Acts, Luke gives us some of the "story" behind the letters to the Corinthians. By referring to Acts 18, answer the following:

a. When and for how long was Paul in Corinth? Where did he live and what did he do there?

b. What evidence does Acts give that the Corinthian community included Jewish Christians?

c. Where did Paul go after Corinth and with whom?

d. Who joined Aquila and Priscilla after Paul left for Galatia, and how is this man described? Why might he have been seen as a competitor of Paul?

2. What were the issues which caused division among the following groups in Corinth?

a. Women and men

b. Married and unmarried

c. Meat-eaters and vegetarians

d. Followers of Peter (Cephas), of Apollos, of Paul

3. What clues does the letter provide concerning the background of the Corinthians as:

a. predominantly Gentile

b. city people

4. In 1 Corinthians Paul, uses the image of the body of Christ in four different ways. Comment on each one, saying what problems in Corinth Paul was seeking to respond to through this use.

a. Your bodies are members of Christ's body

b. The Eucharist is the body of Christ

c. Though many, we are one body

d. The resurrection of the body

VIDEO

The Church of Corinth

As you view the video, please make note of the following:

1. How did Corinth's geographical location contribute to its growth into a commercial and cultural center?

_____

_____

2. Why were there a large number of Jews in Corinth at Paul's time?

_____

_____

3. What do we know about the social status of the Gentile converts to Christianity?

_____

_____

BREAK
(10 minutes)

LEARNING ACTIVITY

1. The church today experiences conflict over basic issues which are similar or comparable to those that divided the Corinthian church. Choose one of the issues below (or your leader may assign one to your group). Read the appropriate passages and answer these questions:

- What principle does Paul use to guide the Corinthians in dealing with this issue?
- Are there any similar problems in the church today?
- What would be Paul's advice to the church today and why?

a. Matters of leadership and authority (Read 1 Cor 1:11-17; 1:26—2:5; 3:1-13, 21-23; 4:1-10)

b. Questions about sexual morality (Read 1 Cor 5:1-5; 6:12-20)

c. Questions about which are the more desirable spiritual gifts (Read 1 Cor 1:4-9; 12:4-11, 27-31; 14:1-33, 37-40)

2. Paul uses the image of the body of Christ to heal the divisions in Corinth. He culminates the use of this image with a description of the resurrection in 1 Cor 15. Read 1 Cor 15:50-58. How can belief in the resurrection help heal the divisions in the church in Corinth?

FAITH SHARING

1. Like the church in Corinth, the church today also experiences divisions and disagreements. What effects does the existence of such divisions or disagreements have on you? Give an example.

2. What in Paul's first letter to the Corinthians do you find helpful in dealing with such problems?

3. In what ways does Paul's advice call you to change?

CLOSING PRAYER

Hearing the Word

Leader:
Let us pray in silence as we contemplate Christ crucified.

(Brief pause)

Reading:
1 Cor 1:21-25

Breaking of the Bread

Leader:
It is the body of Christ, crucified and risen, that we celebrate at Eucharist, that we become at Eucharist. As we break and share the bread, please offer a prayer of thanksgiving for a sign of hope in our world, in the church, or in your life.

Sharing of the Cup

Leader:
As we drink this cup, please offer a prayer of petition for those who suffer in our world, in the church, or in your life.

Song

Blessing

Leader:
May the favor of the Lord Jesus be with you.

All:
And also with you.

FOLLOW-UP

A. Journaling

Read 1 Cor 11:1; 9:19-27. Think again of Paul's use of himself and his own experience as a way of encouraging the Corinthians. Also consider his use of the image of the body of Christ and the contexts in which he uses this image. Write a prayer or reflection expressing your gratitude for participation in the body of Christ and acknowledging your responsibility to live as part of it. Do you perceive your faith-life as public witness? Do you ever feel you are too timid or interior about faith?

B. Additional Resources

1. Read Joseph P. Fitzpatrick, S.J., *Paul: Saint of the Inner City*, Chapter 4, "Corinth," pp. 39-57.

2. Read *The Catholic Study Bible*, 1 Corinthians, RG 485-495, and the introduction to 1 Corinthians in this or another New American Bible.

3. a. Using the Hammond *Atlas of the Bible Lands*, examine the maps on pp. 32-33. Locate Corinth. Why is this such a prominent city in the ancient world? What would be its strategic importance for the spread of Christianity?

b. Find the following geographic references mentioned in Acts 18:1-22: Athens, Pontus, Macedonia, Syria, Cenchreae, Ephesus, Caesarea.

c. Study the maps in Perkins, pp. 176 and 183.

5. 2 Corinthians

Preparation

- Read Perkins, Chapter 10, pp. 186-190 and study the outline of 2 Corinthians, p. 187.
- Read 2 Corinthians.
- The following will be the focus of this session:
  — 2 Cor 5:17-20; 2 Cor 10-13: The ministry of reconciliation; see also 2 Cor 10:1—13:10
  — 2 Cor 3: The ministry of the new covenant
  — 2 Cor 8 and 9: The significance of the collection; see also 1 Cor 16:1-4 and Rom 15:25-29.
- Reflect on the FOCUS statement and REVIEW OF CONTENTS questions.

FOCUS

Although Paul was quite familiar with the Corinthians, this very familiarity seems to have been a source of difficulty between him and them. There were other leaders whom the Corinthians apparently preferred to Paul, among them, Peter, Apollos and Titus. Paul admitted to a lack of speaking skills and an unimpressive appearance. That he supported himself by working with his hands also raised questions among the Corinthians about his apostleship.

2 Corinthians is actually a composite of several letters Paul wrote to the Corinthians. Although these dealt with different issues, together they represent the

apostle's continued attempt to challenge the Corinthians' values, to call them to conversion and reconciliation, and to encourage them to create among themselves a community worthy of the name "church." Of all of Paul's letters, 2 Corinthians gives us the most personal expression of Paul's own sentiments and vulnerability. Clearly, Paul had many opponents in Corinth. Yet, in his writings, his tone is affectionate and his purpose conciliatory.

In this session we will study 2 Corinthians in its final form, focusing on what this letter says about reconciliation, about the new covenant, and about Paul's view of the theological basis for the collection for the poor in Jerusalem.

OPENING PRAYER

Call to Prayer

Leader:
Grace and peace from God our Father and the Lord Jesus Christ.

All:
And also with you.

Paul Speaks to Us

Reading:
2 Cor 4:5-10

Song

REVIEW OF CONTENTS

1. Study the outline of 2 Corinthians (p. 187).

a. Identify the three parts of an ancient Greek letter: the introduction or address, the body, and the conclusion.

b. Compare the greetings of 1 Cor 1:1-3 and 2 Cor 1:1-2. What are the similarities? Differences?

c. There are three parts to the body of this letter. What are they?

d. 2 Corinthians was written in response to a crisis of confidence between Paul and the Corinthians. In 1:12—7:16 Paul treats the crisis in three parts. Where are these parts and what is the topic of each?

2. Review 2 Cor 1:12—2:13 on Paul's change of plans and the problems it caused.

a. What had Paul promised to do but did not do?

b. Why did Paul change his plans?

c. What criticism did the Corinthians make when Paul changed his mind? Why was this situation so painful to both Paul and to the Corinthians?

3. Read 2 Cor 3 where Paul contrasts his ministry of the "new covenant" with Moses' ministry of the "old covenant" (2 Cor 3:14)

a. How does Paul say his ministry is superior to that of Moses?

b. Using the notes of the NAB, identify the Old Testament sources of Paul's contrast between the old and new covenant.

4. Read 2 Cor 4:7-18 where Paul describes the paradox of ministry. Wherein lies the paradox? What experiences does Paul allude to in order to show the surpassing power of God?

5. Read 2 Cor 5:11-21. How does Paul describe Christ's role in the world? What does God tell us in Christ? How does Paul describe those who are "in Christ"?

VIDEO

Second Corinthians: Division and Reconciliation

As you view the video, please make note of the following:

1. Who were the "superlative apostles" whose authority was being used by factions who challenged Paul in Corinth?

_____

_____

2. Complete the following sentences to show how Paul defends his authority in 2 Corinthians:

a. Paul's preaching is founded not on the earthly Jesus but on _____.

b. Paul's ministry does not rely on external letters of recommendation, but on _____.

c. Though unskilled in speech, Paul has _____.

d. Paul preaches not himself, but _____.

BREAK
(10 minutes)

LEARNING ACTIVITY

1. It is generally assumed that Paul originally wrote several letters to the Corinthians and that 2 Corinthians is a "composite letter," i.e., it was compiled by editing together parts of these letters.

a. You will note from reading the passages below in their immediate contexts that the transitions are abrupt or non-existent. In each instance, it appears that there is some interruption and that originally this segment did not belong where we find it now. Explain the incongruity of each of these:

2 Cor 2:12-13
2 Cor 6:11—7:1
2 Cor 7:2-5
2 Cor 9:1-3
2 Cor 10:1-3

b. Now that you have studied the transitions, can you find four letters?

2. Your group should choose to do either A (chapters 1-7), B (chapters 8-9), or C (chapters 10-13) below. Look over these sections and answer the questions appropriate to your choice of passages.

Group A: Chapters 1-7

1. Name some of the many criticisms the Corinthians have of Paul that you know from this letter and from having read and studied 1 Corinthians.

2. How is the present crisis resolved?

3. Paul tells the Corinthians in 2 Cor 5:17-20 to become "ambassadors of reconciliation." Paul himself has been called the "apostle of reconciliation" Do you think this is appropriate and why?

Group B: Chapters 8-9

1. Chapters 8 and 9 seem to have originally been two separate notes about the collection. What does Paul say in 8:1-5 about the Macedonian churches? How does he reverse this in 9:2?

2. Why is the abundance and generosity of the collection so important to Paul (See also 1 Cor 16:1-4 and Rom 15:25-29)?

3. What is Titus's role and why is it required (8:16-24)?

Group C: Chapters 10-13

1. What indications can you find that 2 Cor 10-13 may be the so-called "letter of tears" referred to in 2 Cor 2:4?

2. Chapters 10-13 present Paul's defense of his ministry. How does this image of the "earthen vessel" (2 Cor 4:7) help you better understand what Paul says in 11:21-29 and 12:1-10 (also 6:3-10)? What is Paul reacting to in this emotional defense of his ministry?

3. Reflect for a moment on Paul's sharing of his own weaknesses as a way to relate to the Corinthians' concerns and to emphasize his own authority as an apostle. What do you think of this? Is it too personal or not personal enough? Why? Is this a good strategy for bringing about a change of heart on the part of the Corinthians?

The temple of Apollo in Corinth. Only 7 of the 38 columns which Paul would have seen are still standing.

FAITH SHARING

Continuing in the same small groups, answer as many of these questions as your have time for.

1. Read 2 Cor 4:5-18 and share your responses to the following:

a. How does the ministry of preaching "not ourselves but Jesus Christ" embolden and change us?

b. What does the image of a "treasure in earthen vessels" mean to you?

2. Read 2 Cor 5:11-21 and share your responses to the following:

a. What does the phrase in 5:14, "For the love of God impels us," mean in your life?

b. How can God be appealing through us to the world to be reconciled?

CLOSING PRAYER

Hearing the Word

Leader:
Praised be God, the Father of our Lord Jesus Christ, the Father of mercies, and the God of all consolation. God comforts us in our afflictions and thus enables us to com-

fort those who are in trouble, with the same consolation we have received from him. (2 Cor 1:3-4)

(Brief silence)

Reading
2 Cor 5:17-18

Blessing for Reconciliation

Leader:
God chose us, human, earthen vessels, to be the ministers of reconciliation. Let us bless each other, then, for this ministry.

Leader:
(Name), you are an ambassador for Christ. Be reconciled to God.
(The blessing is then passed along through the group.)

Leader:
Confident that God is the source of reconciliation and healing, we join hands and pray in the words Jesus taught us.

All:
Our Father . . .

Leader:
The grace of the Lord Jesus Christ and the love of God and the fellowship of the Holy Spirit be with you all.

All:
And also with you.

FOLLOW-UP

A. Journaling

Reread 2 Cor 4:7-11. Write a meditation or prayer in which you express your own personal experience of holding a treasure in an earthen vessel. Are you more concerned about the vessel than the treasure? Do you sufficiently value the treasure? Note that Paul insists in the surrounding context that we must not be discouraged (see 4:1, 16). Include in your prayer recognition of the grace of courage and perseverance and your need to keep the source of this grace always in mind.

B. Additional Resources

1. Read *The Catholic Study Bible*, 2 Corinthians, RG 496-503, and the introduction to 2 Corinthians in this or another New American Bible.

2. Using the Hammond *Atlas of the Bible Lands*, locate Corinth on p. 33. Note its distance from Ephesus where Paul went when he left that city. Find Achaia, the province in which Corinth is located. Paul probably wrote 2 Corinthians from Macedonia. Find Macedonia on the map.

6. Galatians

Preparation

- Read Perkins, Chapter 9, pp. 160-168.
- Read Paul's letter to the Galatians and Acts 8:4-8, 14-17; 10:1-49; 11:1-18; 13:13-14, 15:1-34; 16:6; 18:23.
- Reflect on the FOCUS statement and REVIEW OF CONTENTS questions.

FOCUS

One of the most important and painful problems of the early church was resolving the terms under which the Gentiles were admitted. Acts tells us of how, before Paul, Stephen and even Peter were involved in the conversion of the Gentiles. Paul insists in Galatians that there is only one gospel, not one for Jews and another for Gentiles. If Jews were freely admitted and given access to grace, then Gentiles also had no other entrance requirement than faith. Paul opposes the "Judaizers" who insist that the Gentiles should supplement their faith in Jesus Christ with at least the minimal requirements of the Jewish law, including circumcision.

In this session we will study the epistle to the Galatians, focusing on three areas: Paul's argument against any Judaizing tendency, and against Peter and the emissaries of James; Paul's use of the Old Testament scriptures; and Paul's appeal to the Galatians' experience of the Spirit, of freedom and of community. We will learn about the background of the region called Galatia and share our faith on the relationship we find between love and the law.

OPENING PRAYER

Call to Prayer

Leader:
I wish you the favor and peace of God our Father and of the Lord Jesus Christ, who gave himself for our sins.

All:
And the favor and peace of God be with you.

Paul Speaks to Us

Reading:
Galatians 1:11-17

All:
Your hands have made me and fashioned me.
Give me discernment that I may learn your commands.

Let my heart be blameless in your statutes
that I may not be put to shame. (Ps 119:73 and 80)

Leader:
God, whose binding law is generous love, prepare us to receive your word today (tonight). May it lead us beyond the limitations of our own set ways and into your infinite goodness. We ask this through Christ Jesus who makes it possible for us to receive the promised Spirit through faith (Gal 3:14).

All:
Amen.

The area of Pisidian Antioch in Galatia, with the Roman aqueduct in the distance.

REVIEW OF CONTENTS

1. Review Gal 1:1-2:21 where Paul recounts his own call and mission and his confrontation with Peter. Then discuss the following:

a. Why does Paul stress the divine origin of his call and his preaching?

b. Why does Paul stress his Jewish background?

c. In Acts 15:1-34 Luke describes the Council of Jerusalem, around the year 50. What were the issues and outcome there? Who accompanied Paul?

d. According to Galatians, with whom did Paul meet? Who is Kephas? Why does Paul accuse Peter of hypocrisy?

2. Look again at Gal 4:8-20 and 5:1-11.

a. What do 4:8-9 tell us about the background of the Galatians?

b. According to 4:10, what practices are the Galatians engaging in? What other practice is Paul opposed to in Galatians?

c. How does Paul describe his relationship to the Galatians in 4:12-20?

3. Read the conclusion of the letter: 6:11-18.

a. What does 6:11 tell us about the composition of this letter?

b. What does 6:17 tell us about Paul as he writes this letter?

VIDEO

The Church in Galatia

As you view the video, please make note of the following:

1. Why is it difficult to know specifically who the Galatians were?

_____

_____

2. What was the religious background of the Galatians prior to their becoming Christians?

_____

_____

3. Why does Paul tell the story of his conversion to the Galatians?

_____

_____

BREAK
(10 minutes)

LEARNING ACTIVITY

In your groups, choose one of the following topics (or your leader may assign one to you) and respond to the discussion points related to this topic.

1. Justification by faith

a. What does Paul mean by the expression: "Justified by faith in Christ and not by the law" (2:16)?

b. In Gal 3:6-22 Paul links justification and faith through his reading of the Old Testament. How does Paul relate Abraham to the notion of "justification by faith"?

c. What three scriptural arguments does Paul give in Gal 3:16-20 for the superiority of the promise and faith over the law?

d. Read Gal 4:22-31. How is the image of Abraham and his two sons adapted to contrast Judaism and those who are in Christ?

2. Baptism and the cross

Galatians is important for the theology of baptism and the theology of the cross. Read Gal 3:1-5, 10-14, and 27-29 and answer the following questions:

a. For the Greeks, knowledge or wisdom comes through the senses; the highest goods are spiritual. In light of this general philosophical bias, why does Paul call the Galatians "stupid" (3:1)?

b. What does Paul mean by the expression: "After beginning with the Spirit are you now ending with the flesh?" (3:3)?

c. Paul connects a quotation from Dt 27:26 and Dt 21:23 by the key word "curse." What is the curse of the law and how does it affect Jesus and Paul's thinking about the cross?

d. In Gal 3:28, Paul quotes an early Christian baptismal formula to stress the unity of all who are baptized. How do Christians show that they belong to Christ and how are they linked to Abraham? What divisions are overcome through baptism according to this ancient statement of faith?

3. The Spirit and Freedom

The community life of the Galatians is characterized by the Spirit and by freedom. Paul opposes the notion that fulfilling the Jewish law is a condition for the Gentiles' entry into the church. At the same time, it is clear that Paul is not suggesting that the Christians do anything they please.

a. What does Paul mean by the expression: "For freedom Christ set us free, so stand firm and do not submit again to the yoke of slavery" (5:1)?

b. What does Paul himself say in Gal 5:13-26 that would correct the notion that he preaches a law-free gospel?

c. How would you interpret Gal 5:11?

d. In Gal 5:19-23, Paul borrows lists of virtues and vices, probably from Stoic philosophers, on how to live in a "commonwealth," the Stoic image behind Paul's description of the church as the "Body of Christ." What does Paul mean when he says of the gifts of the Spirit, "Against these things there can be no law"?

FAITH SHARING

1. In 5:14 Paul says "The whole law is fulfilled in one statement, namely, 'You shall love your neighbor as yourself.'" Do you find that fulfilling this command is a freeing experience for you? How?

2. Perhaps you remember learning the gifts of the Spirit enumerated in Is 11:2. Find this list and read it aloud. Reflect on these gifts and on the fruits named in Gal 5:22. Which gifts or fruits do you feel you possess? Which would you like to exemplify more?

CLOSING PRAYER

Hearing the Word

Leader:
Let us reflect in silence on those who suffer today because of the restrictions of the law: in our society, throughout the world, and even in the church. (Allow a few moments of silence.)

First Reading:
Rom 5:8-11

(Silent Reflection)

Second Reading:
Gal 3:23-28

(Silent Reflection)

Shared Prayer

Leader:
Let us pray for all those who suffer today because of the law of religions, societies or governments. Our response to the prayer will be: God of faith, renew us in your promise.

(Petitions are now offered.)

Leader:
It was for liberty that Christ freed us. God of liberty, help us to stand firm in our faith. Forgive us for the times that we have bound others to laws and rules which inhibited growth. Free us for the faith that expresses itself through love. May your peace and mercy be on all who follow this rule of life and on the Israel of God.

All:
Amen.

Leader:
May the favor of our Lord Jesus Christ be with your spirit.

All:
And also with you.

FOLLOW-UP

A. Journaling

Galatians is the only epistle of Paul that lacks a thanksgiving. In his haste to correct the errors of the Galatians, Paul omits this part of his letter. The classical letter writers before Paul normally referred to personal gifts of health and prosperity for which they thanked the deities. Read the thanksgiving in Rom 1:8-15 for inspiration and to see how Paul adapts this ancient letter form, thanking God for the graces his addressees enjoy rather than for those Paul himself experiences. Reflecting upon all the graces given to you personally, your loved ones, members of this Bible study group, or other friends, write a thanksgiving to close out this session.

B. Additional Resources

1. Read *The Catholic Study Bible*, Galatians, RG 503-509 and the introduction to Galatians in this or another NAB.

2. a. Using the maps on pp. 32-33 in the Hammond *Atlas of the Bible Lands*, trace Paul's second and third missionary journeys through the province of Galatia.

b. The following places are possible destinations for the letter to the Galatians: Ancyra, Pisidia, Iconium, Pamphilia, Pisidian Antioch, Lystra, Derbe. Find them on the map on p. 33.

7. Romans

Preparation

- Read Perkins, chapter 9, pp. 168-174.
- Read Paul's letter to the Romans. The following passages will be studied in this session:
  — The address and conclusion: Rom 1:1-15; 15:14—16:27
  — The theme of the epistle: Rom 1:16-17
  — The universality of sin: Rom 1:18—3:31; 5:12-21; 7:13-25
  — All have access to justification through faith: Rom 4:1-12; 6:1-11; 8:18-39
  — All Israel will be saved: Rom 9:1-5; 10:1-4; 11:1-5
  — The church, community of the justified: Rom 12:1-21; 14:1—15:13
- Read Acts 25:1—28:31
- Reflect on the FOCUS statement and REVIEW OF CONTENTS questions.

FOCUS

It is not known who founded the Roman church, but it was not Paul. Tradition holds that it was Peter, and the epistle clearly states that the faith of the Romans was well known throughout the world. Although Paul had not been to Rome, he had long desired to go. Perhaps more than any other epistle, Romans shows that Paul's mission was not an individual affair. Paul was dependent on the Romans and on his reception there so that he could proceed with his missionary plans. In his epistle, he speaks as though he is confident that he and the Romans share a common faith and gospel. His entire work will be jeopardized if he and the Romans do not believe one and the same gospel.

In this session we will study the epistle to the Romans, the most developed, objective statement of the principal tenets of Paul's gospel. In Romans, Paul defines the gospel not as a story about Jesus but as "the power to save all who believe, Jews or Gentiles." We will consider the three major parts of the body of the letter: Paul's doctrine on universal sin and universal salvation; the role of Israel in God's plan of salvation; Paul's exhortation to believers to practice their faith. The video will provide us with background on the Christian community in Rome. During the faith sharing segment we will try to compose our own statement of the gospel as Paul does in Rom 1:16-17 and share that together.

OPENING PRAYER

Call to Prayer

Leader:
Grace and peace from God and the Lord Jesus Christ.

All:
And also with you.

Leader:
We are not ashamed of the gospel. It is the power of God leading everyone who believes in it to salvation, the Jew first, and then the Greek. For in the gospel is revealed the justice of God which begins and ends with faith; as Scripture says, "The just shall live by faith." (Rom 1:16-17)
Let us pray:

All:
God, show your faithfulness,
bless us, and make your face shine upon us!

For the earth will acknowledge your ways,
and all the nations will know your power to save.

May all the nations praise you O God;
may all the nations praise you! (Ps 67:1-3)

Paul Speaks to Us

Leader:
Let us be attentive to the revelation of God through the words of Paul and the experience of our faith.

Reading:
Rom 11:33-36

All:
(Repeat Ps 67:1-3.)

REVIEW OF CONTENTS

1. Describe the situation in Paul's life as he writes Romans. What were his plans and expectations? How did those plans turn out?

2. What do the following tell us about the life of the church in Rome?

a. The return of Prisca and Aquila to Rome from Corinth (cf. Rom 16:3-4 and Acts 18:1-2).

b. Paul's command that Christians in Rome pay taxes (cf. 13:1-7).

c. Disputes among the Christians about which foods may be eaten and which feasts should be observed (cf. 14:1-12).

3. Romans provides a clear example of the ancient letter form. Using the outline in Perkins on pp. 170-171 or the headings in your Bible, identify the three major parts.

Address
Body
Conclusion

4. The body of the epistle may be further divided into three parts: chapters 1:16—8:39; chapters 9-11, chapters 12:1—15:13. What is the major theme of each of these parts?

VIDEO

Romans: Jewish and Gentile Christians

As you view the video please make note of the following:

1. Why is Romans unique among Paul's letters?

_____

_____

2. What was the status of Jews in Rome?

_____

_____

3. What was the status of Christianity in Rome at the time of Paul's letter?

_____

_____

BREAK
(10 minutes)

LEARNING ACTIVITY

In the review of contents we saw that the body of Romans is divided into three parts: chapters 1:16—8:39; chapters 9-11, and chapters 12:1—15:13. Choose one of the following sets of questions (or your leader may assign one to your group). When finished, one member of each group may report back to the whole.

Group A

Look closely at the first eight chapters and respond to the following questions:

1. In Rom 1:16—8:39, Paul states the universal need for salvation, called "sin," in three ways: can you identify them in the following passages?

a. Rom 1:18—3:31

b. Rom 5:12-21

c. Rom 7:19-21

2. In Rom 1:16—8:39, Paul insists on the universality of salvation through faith. Look at the following passages and name three ways in which Paul shows that all are saved through faith.

a. Rom 4

b. Rom 5:1-11

c. Rom 8:18-39

Group B

Rom 9–11 takes up the question which was so painful in the early church, about the Jews' rejection of the gospel even while the Gentiles were accepting it. Look over this passage and find answers to the following questions.

1. Read Rom 9:1-5; 10:1-2; 11:1-5. Some think that in chapters 9–11, Paul is defending himself against the charge that he is a renegade Jew, disloyal to his own people. What are some of the indications in these passages that Paul remains faithful to his Jewish heritage?

2. In Rom 9–11, Paul makes abundant use of the Old Testament. Find at least one example of how Paul draws on the Old Testament to support the following statements:

a. "All of Israel are not Israel." (Rom 9:6)

b. "Has God rejected his people? Of course not!" (11:1)

3. Finally, in the concluding hymn of 11:33-36, how does Paul "resolve" the question of Israel's salvation?

Group C

Rom 12–15 contains the parenesis or application of ethical reflections to the situation of the church in Rome. We have stressed that Paul manifests two concerns in all his writings—Christians' relationships with outsiders and their relationships among themselves.

1. Looking especially at Rom 12–13, what are some suggestions Paul makes concerning relations with outsiders and what do these imply about the role of Christians in the larger Roman society?

2. Look at 12:9-21 and 13:8-10 where Paul develops the responsibilities of the love command. Which verses suggest that Paul is speaking to persecuted Christians? Are there sayings of Jesus echoed here?

3. Consider 12:20-21 and see the NAB note on the Old Testament source of 12:20. What does this mean? How could this be part of Paul's mission strategy?

4. Study especially Rom 14:1—15:13 for information on some of the difficulties Roman Christians had among themselves. What are some of these?

The temple of Saturn in the Roman Forum.

FAITH SHARING

In Rom 1:16-17 Paul summarizes the gospel he preaches in this way: For I am not ashamed of the gospel. It is the power of God for the salvation of everyone who believes: for Jew first, and then Greek. For in it is revealed the righteousness of God from faith to faith; as it is written, "The one who is righteous by faith shall live."

Based on your study of Paul (and the gospels) write a brief summary of the gospel you believe and live. Share this with your group.

_____

_____

_____

_____

CLOSING PRAYER

Call to Prayer

Leader:
The element of bread is a universal symbol of nourishment and sustenance. When it is broken before the family or community that is gathered at the table, it is a reminder of human brokenness and the need to share our lives through that brokenness.

Today we gather to share the bread of the Middle East, a place where pilgrims of many religions travel to know their roots and traditions, a place where today, as in Paul's time, peoples from various religious traditions quarrel and go to war as attempts to justify one belief over another, or one's rights to the land over another.

We will break the bread, dip it in the bitter herbs, and remember the brokenness and sin that keep us from justice and true faith.

Hearing the Word

First Reading:
Rom 11:30-32

Shared Prayer

Leader:
We know that with God all things are possible. "Despite the increase of sin, grace has far surpassed it, so that, as sin reigned through death, grace may reign by way of justice leading to eternal life, through Jesus Christ, our Lord." (Rom 5:20-21)

We again break bread and dip it in honey as a sign of God's grace which empowers us to do justice with faith.

Hearing the Word

Second Reading:
Rom 12:9-16

Shared Prayer

Our Father...

Leader:
May God, the source of hope, fill you with all joy and
peace in believing so that through the power of the Holy
Spirit you may have hope in abundance (15:13).

All:
Amen

FOLLOW-UP

A. Journaling

Reflect again on the statement of the gospel you composed during the faith sharing time. Having shared and reflected on it, how would you like to expand or refine it?

B. Additional Resources

1. Read *The Catholic Study Bible*, Romans RG 472-484 and the introduction to Romans in this or another NAB.

2. Using the Hammond *Atlas of the Bible Lands*, pp. 33 and 36, locate Rome. Under what circumstances did Paul go there? Trace his journey, locating the following cities along the way: Caesarea, Myra and Cnidus in Lycia, the islands of Crete and Malta.

3. Read Joseph P. Fitzpatrick, S.J., *Paul, Saint of the Inner City*, chapter 6, "Rome," pp. 68-86.

8. Colossians and Ephesians

Preparation

- Read Perkins, Chapter 11, pp. 191-202.
- Review Chapter 6, pp. 98-113 and Session 5, "The Beginnings of Christology" in the Paulist Bible Study Program unit *Jesus and the Gospels*.
- Read the letter to the Colossians and the following selections from the letter to the Ephesians:
  — The church as Christ's body: Eph 1:18-23; 4:11-16
  — Unity in Christ: Eph 2:11-22
  — Appropriate conduct of Christians: Eph 4:25—5:1; 5:15—6:9
- Read Acts 19; 1 Cor 15:32
- Reflect on the FOCUS statement and REVIEW OF CONTENTS questions.

FOCUS

In this session we will seek to get an overview of the epistles to the Colossians and to the Ephesians. We will note how Paul's thinking on the church and on the role of Christ progressed. In the early letters, Paul focused on specific questions about Christ's death, resurrection, and return. The church was presented as a concrete, local reality. In these letters Christ is presented as the cosmic, triumphant Lord of all creation and the church is seen as a spiritual and universal reality. As we will see, this is one reason why many believe Paul himself did not actually write these letters.

We will also consider the moral exhortation to Christians contained in these letters, particularly their focus on the household. The video portion will present further background on the life of the church in the urban centers of Colossae and Ephesus. Finally, as we bring this unit to a close, we will have the opportunity to reflect and share our faith on how we have grown through this study of Paul and his letters.

OPENING PRAYER

Call to Prayer

Leader:
Grace be with all who love our Lord Jesus Christ with unfailing love.

All:
And also with you.

Paul Speaks to Us

Leader:
Let us pray.

All:

Praised be the God and Father
of our Lord Jesus Christ, who has bestowed on us in
    Christ
every spiritual blessing in the heavens.

God chose us in him
before the world began
to be holy and blameless in his sight.

God predestined us
to be his adopted children through Jesus Christ,
such was his will and pleasure.
that all might praise the glorious favor
he has bestowed on us in his beloved.

In him and through his blood, we have been redeemed,
and our sins forgiven,
so immeasurably generous
is God's favor to us.

God has given us the wisdom
to understand fully the mystery,
the plan he was pleased
to decree in Christ.

A plan to be carried out
in Christ, in the fullness of time,
to bring all things into one in him,
in the heavens and on earth (Eph 1:3-10).

Leader:

God, be with us again as we learn to understand the mystery of your plan.

All:

Amen.

Artemis, the chief goddess of Ephesus. Paul's rejection of her cult provoked a riot among the silversmiths.

REVIEW OF CONTENTS

1. How is the imprisonment referred to in Colossians and Ephesians different from the imprisonment in Philippians and Philemon?

2. a. Using the chart on p. 195 of Perkins, compare these passages in Ephesians with their parallels in Colossians. What similarities do you find?

Eph 1:1-2
Eph 3:1-13
Eph 6:21-22

b. What are some reasons for believing that Ephesians is a ''circular letter'' written for all the churches of Asia Minor?

3. a. What do we learn from Col 2:15-23 about the beliefs of those whom Paul opposed?

b. How does the image of Christ as cosmic, victorious Lord make these beliefs and practices of his opponents obsolete?

4. Compare Col 3:18-19 with Eph 5:21-33.

a. How does Ephesians expand the conventional ''ordering'' of the relationship between husband and wife?

b. How can the term "obey" be read in a positive way?

c. Was anything new demanded of Christian husbands which went beyond what the society of Paul's time required?

VIDEO

Colossians and Ephesians

As you view the video, please make note of the following:

1. Why does Colossians stress Christ as the cosmic Lord?

_____

_____

2. How is the image of the Body of Christ in Ephesians different from this image in the early letters of Paul?

_____

_____

BREAK

(10 minutes)

LEARNING ACTIVITY

1. Christology, that is, different interpretations or images of Christ and his work of redemption, is of course, a primary concern of Paul and his churches. No single image suffices to represent all the ways the saving life, death and resurrection of Christ can be related to the believing community or to individuals who profess to be Christian.

Choose one of the images or cluster of images listed below (or your leader may assign one to your group). Then read the appropriate passages and discuss them. Make note of how the meaning of this image evolves from passage to passage. Compose a brief summary of what this image involves. Someone from each group should read the summary to the larger group at the end of this exercise.

a. Jesus, Lord, or Judge of all Humankind, Reconciling the World to Himself

1 Cor 15:24-28
Col 1:20
Eph 1:7-10, 20-23; 2:16-18

b. Christ, Image of God or Wisdom of God

2 Cor 4:4
Col 1:15
Eph 1:17-18

c. Jesus, Firstborn among Many

Rom 8:29
1 Cor 15:23
Col 1:15

d. The Suffering Christ

Phil 2:5-11
Rom 5:1-11
Col 1:24

If you have time, continue with these questions:

2. We see in a comparison between the early epistles of Paul and these later epistles attributed to Paul a movement away from such concerns as the "day of the Lord" or "end of the world" toward a glorifying of the image of Christ. How do you account for this development?

3. In his early epistles, Paul addressed the specific situation of local churches. As his reflection on the church developed, it became more universally applicable, more cosmic and victorious. What could have been some of the contributing factors to this development?

FAITH SHARING

1. In this unit we have seen that Paul uses a variety of images to describe Christ. Which of these do you feel most at home with? Why? How does this image help you in your daily life as a Christian?

2. We have seen in this session and in this unit how the imagery Paul used to describe Christ evolved as the church grew and changed. How has your own image of Christ evolved because of your participation in this unit of the Paulist Bible Study Program?

3. We have also studied the various images Paul uses for the church. Which of these is most useful for you? How has your image of the church evolved as a result of your study of Paul?

CLOSING PRAYER

Call to Prayer

Leader:
My friends, you are no longer strangers and aliens, but you are fellow citizens with the holy ones and members of the household of God, built upon the foundation of the apostles and prophets, with Christ Jesus as the capstone. Through him the whole structure is held together and grows into a temple sacred in the Lord; in him you also are being built together into a dwelling place of God in the Spirit (Eph 2:19-22).

Let us pray in thanksgiving for the revelation of God through Christ now revealed by the Spirit.

Litany

Reader 1:
To God, the Creator of all,

Response:
To you we offer thanks and praise!

Reader 1:
To Jesus Christ, first born of all creation,

Response:
To you we offer thanks and praise!

Reader 1:
To the Spirit, the origin of peace, who preserves unity,

Response:
To you we offer thanks and praise!

Reader 2:
Continue to create your church as your handiwork, that we may lead a life of good deeds.

Response:
Give us the wisdom to understand fully your mystery.

Reader 2:
In our own flesh, fill up in us what is lacking in the sufferings of Christ, for the sake of the church.

Response:
Enable us to become ambassadors of reconciliation, making peace through the blood of his cross.

Reader 2:
Clothe us in your love, that we may recognize unity in our many gifts.

Response:
Work in us your power which can do immeasurably more than we can ask or imagine.

Leader:
God of faith, in your plan you have called us together to reflect on your word and to learn through your servant, Paul. We have shared and celebrated our faith through our stories of faith, our tradition, and through prayer and ritual. Make us always aware that your word and your presence is as close to us as we are to one another.

Sign of Peace

As our final sign and gesture of praise to you, we offer one another a sign of your peace.

Concluding Song

FOLLOW-UP

A. Journaling

Read Eph 3:7-21 where Paul describes his ministry and tells his readers of his prayer for them. Consider your own ministry. Reflect on the graces given to you and the ways in which you know that God's plan of salvation has been carried out in your life. Write a prayer for a loved one in the spirit of Paul's prayer, or write a meditation expressing gratitude to God for the ways God has accomplished in you "far more than we can ask or imagine."

Also, look back at the learning goals you set for yourself at the beginning of this study of Paul. Are you pleased with the goals you set and your accomplishment of them? What still remains to be done? How would you like to follow up on the study of Paul which you have begun?

B. Additional Resources

1. Read *The Catholic Study Bible*, Ephesians, RG 509-514 and Colossians, RG 518-522, and the introductions to these letters in this or another NAB.

2. Using the Hammond *Atlas of the Bible Lands*, p. 33, find Colossae and Ephesus in Asia Minor.